SCIENCE FACTORY
UNITS &
MEASUREMENTS

JON RICHARDS

FRANKLIN WATTS
LONDON • SYDNEY

Designed and produced by
Aladdin Books Ltd
28 Percy Street
London W1P 0LD

ISBN 0 7496 3434 0

First published in Great Britain
in 2000 by
Franklin Watts Books
96 Leonard Street
London EC2A 4XD

Editor
Kathy Gemmell

Design

David West
Children's Book Design

Designer
Jennifer Skelly

Illustrator
Ian Moores

Printed in Belgium

The author, Jon Richards, has written
a number of science and technology
books for children.

The consultant, Steve Parker,
has worked on over 150 books for
children, mainly on a science theme.

All the photos in this book were
taken by Roger Vlitos.

INTRODUCTION

Everything we do, everything
we see and everywhere we go
can be measured in one kind of
unit or another. Measuring in
units lets you compare one
distance with another, and
helps you work out how far
away, or how heavy, an object
is. It also tells you how long it
takes you to do something. You
can even measure the wind!
Read on and discover a host
of projects to teach you about
measuring.

CONTENTS

YOUR FACTORY

BEFORE YOU START any of the projects, it is important that you learn a few simple rules about the care of your science factory.

● Always keep your hands and the work surfaces clean. Dirt can damage results and ruin a project.

● Read the instructions very carefully before you start each project.

● Make sure you have all the equipment you need for the project (see checklist opposite).

● If you haven't got the right piece of equipment, then improvise. For example, a washing-up liquid bottle will do just as well as a plastic drinks bottle.

● Don't be afraid to make mistakes. Just start again – patience is very important!

Equipment checklist:
- Cocktail sticks and wooden sticks
- Cardboard box and shoe box
- Drinking straws
- Plastic drinks bottles and transparent beakers
- Water, salt, oil and vinegar
- Scissors, sticky tape and glue
- Ruler, protractor and compass
- Small container and large bowl
- Felt-tip pens, pencil and paints
- Measuring jug and food colouring
- Toy car, battery and other small objects
- Paper, stiff card, coloured card and plastic film
- Drawing pins, small tacks, nails and paper fasteners
- Cork, corkboard and piece of wood
- Cotton thread, elastic band and string
- Table-tennis ball
- Modelling clay
- Watch or clock
- Coat hanger

WARNING:
Some of the projects in this book need the help of an adult. Always ask a grown-up to give you a hand when you are using scissors or sharp objects such as nails.

HOW FAR?

HOW FAR DO YOU HAVE TO TRAVEL to school each day? How long is your bedroom? How far away are the shops? All of these questions are about distance. To measure distance, we use units such as centimetres, metres and even kilometres. Build a measuring wheel in this project and see how you can measure the distance between objects.

WHAT YOU NEED
Ruler
String
Drawing pin
Pencil
Coloured card
Nail
Wooden stick
Cork
Sticky tape
Glue

SMALLER WHEEL
Use string just over 8cm long to make another circle about 50cm around its edge. This will give a more exact reading than the first wheel because smaller units are more accurate.

5 *To measure the distance between two objects, start with your wheel next to the first object, with the arrow pointing to the ground. Roll it to the second object in a straight line. Count how many times the arrow touches the ground before you reach the second object – this will give you the distance between the objects in metres.*

MEASURING WHEEL

1 Cut a piece of string that is just over 16cm long. Tie the pencil to one end and pin the other end onto the middle of the piece of card. Then draw a circle using the pencil. Ask an adult to cut out the circle.

2 Cut out an arrow shape and glue it to your circle. Point the tip of the arrow towards the edge of the circle, and the base towards the centre of the circle (where the drawing pin was).

3 Tape the nail across one end of the stick, as shown. Wrap more tape around the stick to hold the first piece of tape in place.

4 Push the nail through the centre of the circle. Push the cork onto the nail. Make sure the wheel can still turn.

WHY IT WORKS

Making the radius of the circle (the distance from the centre to the edge) 16cm makes the distance around the edge 1m. The wheel goes round once for every metre covered. So the number of times it goes round equals the number of metres between the objects.

1 METRE

FINDING THE ANGLE

When mapping out a piece of land, surveyors not only need to find out the distance between points, but also the steepness of any slope, called the gradient. You may have seen surveyors at work using an instrument on a tripod called a theodolite. This tells them the angle, up or down, from where they are standing to another piece of ground. Make a simple theodolite in this project.

What you need
*Coloured card
Glue
Scissors
Ruler
Protractor
Battery
String
Sticky tape*

MEASURING HEIGHT

Surveyors also use theodolites to calculate the height of objects. By finding out the angle to the top of an object and the distance to the object from where they are standing, surveyors use simple mathematics to find out the object's height.

4 *To measure the angle between where you are and another object, simply look at the object through the two viewers. Ask somebody to read off the angle between the string and the centre 0° line of the theodolite. This is the angle between you and the object.*

THEODOLITE

1 *Using the method shown on page 7, draw and cut out a circle of card. Cut it in half. Using the protractor and ruler, mark lines at 10° intervals. Number the lines, from 0° in the middle to 90° at either end of the flat edge.*

90° — — 90°

0°

2 *Make two viewers by rolling two narrow strips of card into loops. Sandwich these loops between the two semicircles of card and glue them all together.*

3 *Ask an adult to help you cover the battery with card, as shown. Tape the battery to a piece of string 60cm long to make a plumb line. Tape the other end of the string to the centre of the flat edge of the semicircle. You have now made a theodolite.*

WHY IT WORKS

As you raise or lower the flat edge to line it up with an object, the plumb line swings to an angle away from the 0° line. This angle is the same as the angle between yourself and the object.

0°

25°

GRID LOCK

ANOTHER MEASUREMENT surveyors often need is the amount of land something covers. This is called the area of an object. Area can be measured in a wide range of units, including acres, hectares, square centimetres, square metres and square kilometres. Some areas are easy to find. For a square, you simply multiply the length of one side by itself. This project shows you how to find the area of simple and complicated shapes.

WHAT YOU NEED
Sheet of plastic film
Ruler
Felt-tip pen
Coloured card
Scissors

SMALLER GRID

Make a grid with squares that are only 0.5cm across and use it to measure the area of shapes. You will find that you can measure the areas more exactly than with the larger-sized grid.

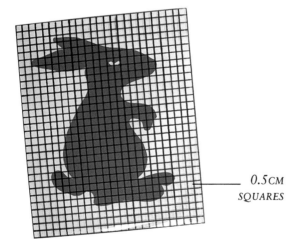

0.5CM SQUARES

FINDING THE AREA

1 *Ask an adult to cut out different shapes from coloured card. Cut out simple shapes such as squares and rectangles, and more complex ones, such as circles or animal shapes.*

2 *Using the ruler and the felt-tip pen, measure centimetre intervals along the edges of the plastic film. Join up opposite points on the edges to form a grid of squares, each 1cm by 1cm.*

WHY IT WORKS

By breaking a shape up into squares, you can see the area it covers. If you ignore the less-than-half-covered squares, you can count each more-than-half-covered square as one full square. Test this by drawing a rectangle and placing the grid over it. Count the squares, then move the grid slightly. Count again, using the rule for partially covered squares. You will get the same result both times.

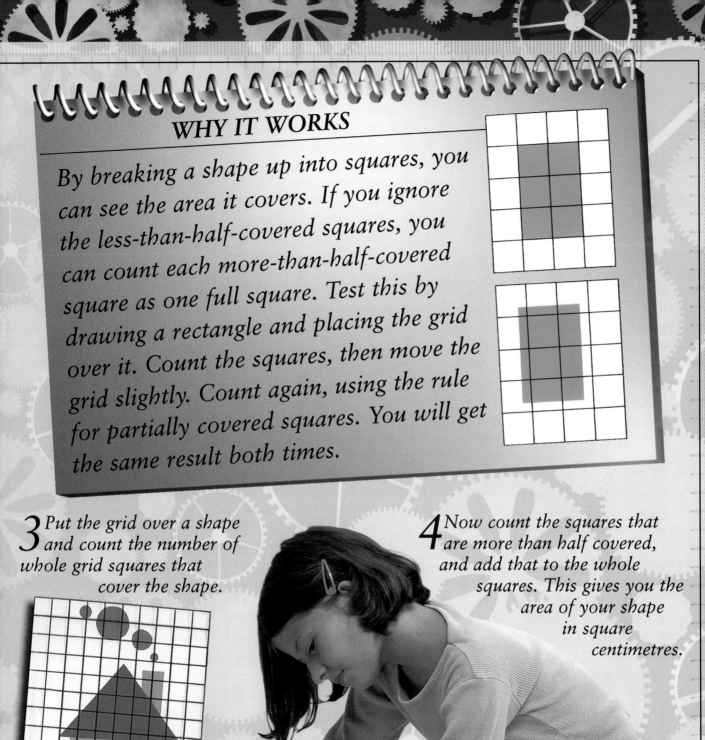

3 Put the grid over a shape and count the number of whole grid squares that cover the shape.

4 Now count the squares that are more than half covered, and add that to the whole squares. This gives you the area of your shape in square centimetres.

SPILLING OVER

WITH DISTANCE AND AREA, you have measured units in one and two dimensions. The amount of space an object takes up in three dimensions is called its volume. As with area, you can use simple maths to work out the volume of some objects – the volume of a box can be found by multiplying its base by its height by its depth. This project shows how to find out the volume of any object.

WHAT YOU NEED
Cardboard box
Scissors
Glue
Coloured card
Two wooden sticks
Small container
Large bowl
· Water
Measuring jug
Small objects

FINDING THE VOLUME

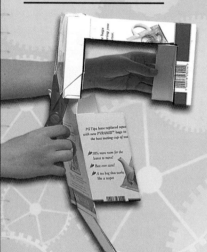

1 *To make a stand, ask an adult to cut out the sides of a cardboard box. The box must be wide enough to slide the large bowl in and out.*

2 *To decorate your stand, cut out strips of coloured card. Glue the strips to the sides and top of the stand.*

3 *Place the sticks over your stand and balance the small container on them. Place the large bowl underneath. Fill the small container to the brim with water. Be careful not to spill water into the large bowl.*

IN THE BATH

With a water-based pen, mark the level of a bath before you get in. As you get in, the level rises. Like the object in the container, your body displaces an amount of water equal to its volume.

4 Gently place an object into the small container.

5 Watch as the water spills over into the large bowl.

6 Pour the water in the large bowl into a measuring jug.

7 Put the jug on a flat surface and read off how much water is in it. This is the volume of the object you put in the container.

WHY IT WORKS

When you place the object into the small container of water, it pushes out, or displaces, a volume of water which equals its own volume. You can then measure this volume of water by pouring it into a measuring jug.

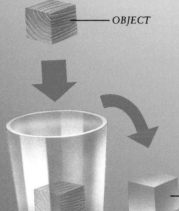

OBJECT

WATER DISPLACED BY OBJECT

FLOATING AND SINKING

WHAT YOU NEED
Drinking straw
Modelling clay
Transparent beakers
Water
Oil
Vinegar
Salt
Felt-tip pen

WHEN A TRAIN IS FULL OF PASSENGERS, we say that the people are closely, or densely, packed inside. In the same way, the tiny molecules which make up substances can be more densely packed in some objects than in others. This project shows you how to make a hydrometer, which allows you to test and compare the densities of different liquids.

HYDROMETER

1 *Ask an adult to cut a length of straw. Put a ball of clay on one end to make a hydrometer.*

2 *Fill a beaker with a certain amount of water. Using the felt-tip pen, mark on the straw the water level at which the straw floats.*

3 *Pour out the same amounts of vinegar, oil and salt water as the original water. Put in the hydrometer and see at what level it floats.*

The density of a liquid depends upon the size of the molecules which make it up, as well as on how tightly packed they are. Oil has big molecules compared to water, but the oil molecules are not as tightly packed together. In fact, they are quite spread out. So water, with its more closely packed molecules, is more dense than oil. The straw will therefore sink further in oil than in water.

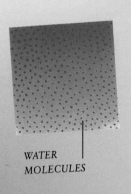

WATER MOLECULES

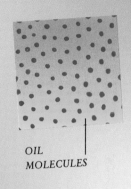

OIL MOLECULES

4 Look at how the hydrometer floats higher in denser liquids, such as salt water, but lower in less dense liquids, such as oil.

SETTLING IN LAYERS

Carefully pour liquids of different densities into the same transparent beaker. They will settle into different bands, with the most dense liquid sitting on the bottom of the beaker and the least dense liquid floating on the top.

LIGHT AND HEAVY

YOU MAY HAVE SEEN HOW ASTRONAUTS in space float around their spacecraft. They have no weight because they are so far from the Earth and moving so fast that they are not affected by its gravity. On the Earth's surface, we feel weight because weight is the combination of the density of an object and the effect of the Earth's gravity. This project shows you how to compare the weight of different objects.

WEIGHING IT UP

1 *Use the ruler and felt-tip pen to mark out a scale along one edge of a strip of card.*

3 *Decorate the top of the plastic bottle using the paints. Ask an adult to cut a small flap into its base. This flap will hold the top of the bottle in place against the piece of wood.*

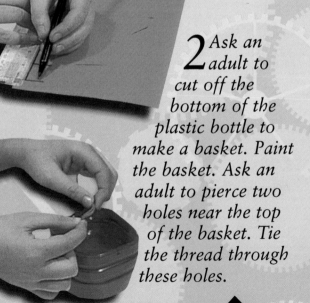

2 *Ask an adult to cut off the bottom of the plastic bottle to make a basket. Paint the basket. Ask an adult to pierce two holes near the top of the basket. Tie the thread through these holes.*

4 *Tie the elastic band to the thread on the basket. Loop the other end of the elastic band over the neck of the bottle. Stick the cocktail stick to the base of the basket to act as a pointer.*

5 Put the piece of wood in an upright position and place the strip of card against it. Ask an adult to secure the top of the bottle to the top of the piece of wood by knocking the two nails through the flap. Mark on the scale where the cocktail stick rests when the basket is empty.

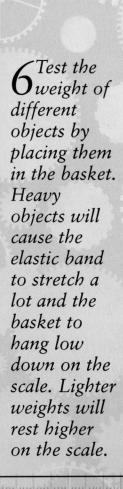

6 Test the weight of different objects by placing them in the basket. Heavy objects will cause the elastic band to stretch a lot and the basket to hang low down on the scale. Lighter weights will rest higher on the scale.

The Earth's gravity attracts objects downwards. The heavier any object placed in the basket is, the more it weighs and the more it stretches the elastic band.

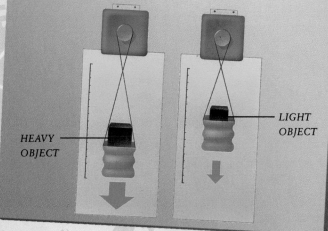

HEAVY OBJECT

LIGHT OBJECT

WEIGHING IN WATER

Take off the elastic band and basket from the bottle top. Put an object in the basket. See how far it stretches the elastic band. Now lower the basket into a bucket of water. What happens to the basket and the elastic band? Is the elastic band still stretched by the same amount?

IN THE BALANCE

WHAT YOU NEED
Two plastic beakers
String
Stiff card
Ruler
Felt-tip pen
Coat hanger
Drinking straw
Sticky tape

THE PREVIOUS PROJECT SHOWED you how to compare the weights of different objects one after the other. But the weight of an object can have another purpose. If you have an object that you know the weight of, you can use it to find the weight of other objects using an instrument called a balance. This project shows you how to make a simple balance.

BALANCING ACT

1 Ask an adult to pierce two holes in each beaker, one on either side near the top. Tie string to these holes to form long hoops.

2 Draw a scale on the card using the felt-tip pen and ruler. Make the central line longer so it stands out.

4 Hang one beaker on each arm of the hanger and check that they are level when the hanger is hung up by its hook. Place the scale behind the hanger so that the middle line sits behind the straw when the beakers are empty.

3 Tape the drinking straw to the underside of the coat hanger so that it points down.

18

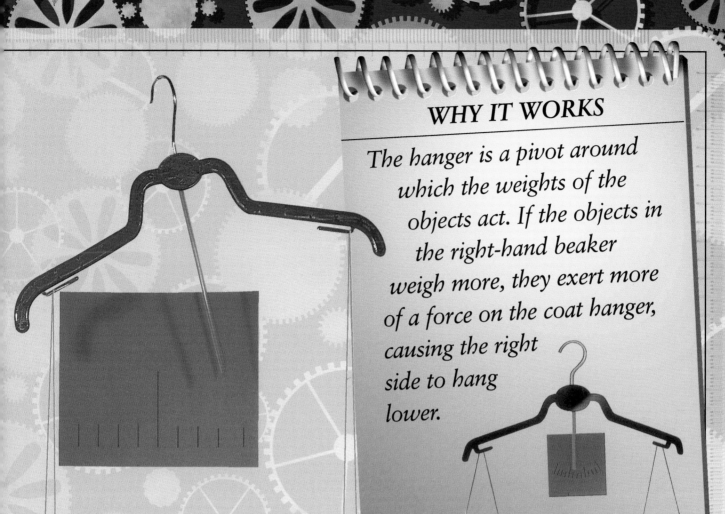

The hanger is a pivot around which the weights of the objects act. If the objects in the right-hand beaker weigh more, they exert more of a force on the coat hanger, causing the right side to hang lower.

RIGHT-HAND BEAKER WEIGHS MORE

5 Compare the weights of different objects by placing them in each basket. See how much you need of different substances before they balance.

COMPARING WEIGHTS

Get two objects which are the same size, but weigh different amounts, such as a tennis ball and a cricket ball. Place them in the beakers. The cricket ball will tip the balance because it is more dense.

FINDING THE MIDDLE

WHAT YOU NEED
Corkboard
Stiff card
Scissors
Drawing pin
String
Modelling clay
Ruler
Pencil

EVERY OBJECT HAS A CENTRE OF GRAVITY. This is an imaginary point through which the weight of the object acts. In the last project, you saw how, by pivoting the coat hanger around its centre of gravity, you were able to make it balance. At any other place, the pivot would not have been in line with the coat hanger's centre of gravity and would not have balanced. This project will show you how to find the centre of gravity for any flat shape.

CENTRE OF GRAVITY

2 *Push one end of a length of string into a lump of modelling clay. Stick the drawing pin through the other end and push it through the card shape. Pin the shape to the corkboard, making sure that it can swing freely.*

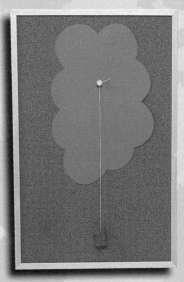

1 *Ask an adult to cut out a random shape from the piece of card.*

5 *Test your shape's centre of gravity by balancing a sharp pencil upright, using modelling clay. Carefully place the shape on the pencil point where the lines cross. The shape will balance.*

WHY IT WORKS

When the string hangs from the same point as the card, it passes through the card's centre of gravity. This is because weight always acts vertically down towards the centre of the Earth.

CENTRE OF GRAVITY

3 Using the ruler, draw along the line made by the string as it hangs. Repeat a few times, pinning the shape in a different place each time.

4 You will notice that the lines cross in one spot. This spot is the shape's centre of gravity.

FANCY SHAPES

Cut out complex shapes from card. Use the same method to find their centre of gravity. Each time you pin the shapes, pin them as close to the edges as you can.

THE SANDS OF TIME

THERE IS A UNIT that is being used continuously and requires measuring all the time – and that's time! For thousands of years, people have measured the passing of time, using more and more complex methods to get more and more accurate readings. One of the earliest forms of time measurer, or clock, was the hourglass. This project shows you how to make your own simple hourglass.

WHAT YOU NEED
Two small bottles
Cardboard
Sharp pencil
Table salt
Watch or clock

HOURGLASS

2 Pour some salt into the other bottle.

1 Make a tube from a strip of cardboard that will fit snugly over the necks of the bottles. Slide it over the top of one bottle. Ask an adult to cut out a small circle of card to cover the mouth of the bottle and to make a small hole in the middle with a sharp pencil. Put the circle inside the tube so that it covers the mouth of the bottle.

3 Turn the bottle with the tube upside down, and slide it over the mouth of the bottle containing the salt. Check that the cardboard tube fits snugly.

4 Turn the bottles over, so that the bottle with the salt is on top. The salt will start pouring into the bottom bottle.

WHY IT WORKS

5 Using a watch or clock, time how long it takes for all the salt to flow from one bottle to the next. When this has happened, turn the bottles over and repeat. You will find that the time is exactly the same.

Gravity makes the salt fall into the bottom bottle. The flow of salt is slowed by the small hole which the salt has to pass through. As the amount of salt and the size of the hole remain the same, the time it takes the salt to flow from one bottle to the next will stay the same however many times you repeat the project.

TIME RUNNING OUT

Make another form of timekeeper using a cardboard funnel, shown here. This time, mark lines on the side of the bottle. Read off where the top of the pile of salt is after each minute.

SWING TIME

TIME IS MEASURED BY SMALLER and smaller units, from years to months to days to hours to seconds and even to millionths of a second. The hourglass you made on pages 22-23 can be useful for measuring periods of time of about a minute, but it doesn't work for very small periods of time. One solution is to use a pendulum clock. This relies on the regular swing of a weight on the end of a length of string or wire, called a pendulum.

WHAT YOU NEED
Cardboard box
Wooden sticks
Card
Modelling clay
Sticky tape
Small tack
Drinking straw
Paints

TICK TOCK

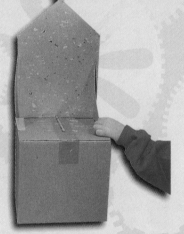

3 Decorate your clock. Mark a scale on the clock face so that you can check the pendulum's swing.

1 Ask an adult to make a hole in the middle of one side of the cardboard box, as shown. Draw and then cut out a clock face the same width as the box.

2 Tape the face to the side of the box. Ask an adult to push a small length of stick through the base of the face. Tape the rest of the stick to the box.

6 Make a pointer from a length of straw and a triangle of card. Ask an adult to fix the pointer to the top of the pendulum.

4 For the pendulum, attach a circle of card and a lump of modelling clay to one end of a long stick.

5 On the other end, attach a short length of stick with a circle of card stuck to each end.

24

7 Ask an adult to tack the pendulum to the piece of wood sticking out from the clock face. Put the clock on the edge of a table so the pendulum swings freely.

WHY IT WORKS

The length of time a pendulum takes to swing is determined by the length of the string or, in this case, the stick. As the pendulum swings, friction from the air and friction on the pivot tack slow the movement and also lessen the distance of each swing. As a result, each swing takes the same amount of time, no matter what distance the pendulum swings.

8 Swing the pendulum. Each swing takes the same time, no matter how far the pendulum moves.

TIME YOUR SWING

The swing time of your pendulum is governed by the length of the wooden stick. If the stick is shorter, it will swing faster, and if it is longer, it will swing slower. Alter the length of the stick, so that each swing takes one second. Check with a watch.

MEASURING SPEED

WHAT YOU NEED
Compass
Felt-tip pen
Stiff card
Scissors
Table-tennis ball
Drawing pin
Sticky tape

THE SPEED OF THINGS is referred to in several places in this book. In the previous project, the speed of the pendulum as it swings is an important factor in determining how long each swing takes. Speed is the rate at which a distance is covered. This project shows how you can compare the different speeds of the air as it moves around you – what we call wind.

WIND SPEED

1 *Draw a curved scale onto card using the compass and the felt-tip pen. Mark equal points on the scale, so that you can compare wind speeds.*

2 *Ask an adult to cut out a strip of card with a small window in it, so that you can see the scale.*

WATCH THE WIND BLOW

Make another wind-speed measurer by tying strips of thick card, thin card, tin foil, paper and tissue paper to a stick, in that order. Start with the thick card at the bottom. A weak wind will only move the tissue paper, but it will take a strong wind to move all the strips, including the thick card.

3 *Tape the table-tennis ball to one end of the card strip. Pin the other end of the strip onto the sheet of card on the spot where the point of the compass made a small hole. Make sure that the strip can swing freely.*

26

4 Hold your wind-speed reader in a windy spot and see how far the cardboard strip is pushed when the wind blows.

WHY IT WORKS

When the wind blows on the table-tennis ball, the moving air pushes the ball. The faster the wind blows, the more the table-tennis ball is pushed, and the further up the scale the cardboard arm moves.

WIND ——————

GETTING FASTER

WHAT YOU NEED
Toy car
Shoe box
Stiff card
Scissors
Plastic bottle
Paper fastener
Paper
Sticky tape
Protractor
Ruler
Felt-tip pen
Food colouring
Water

FROM THE PREVIOUS PROJECT you will have seen that the wind can blow at different speeds. This change of speed is called acceleration if it is getting faster, and deceleration if it is getting slower. This project shows you how different rates of acceleration can be caused by changes in the angle of a slope.

FASTER AND FASTER

1 *Ask an adult to cut out a strip of stiff card to make the ramp. Make sure that the ramp is as wide as the shoe box. Fasten a small piece of card to the ramp to form a catch.*

2 *Tape one end of the ramp to one end of the box, making sure that the ramp can be put at different angles.*

3 *Ask an adult to cut out a quarter circle from card. With a ruler, protractor and felt-tip pen, mark every 10°. Cut small slits at each mark. Slot the catch into one of the slits.*

4 *Ask an adult to cut off the top of a plastic bottle and pierce a small hole in the lid. Cut a hole in a piece of card to hold the upturned bottle top. Tape the card to the top of the car. Tape over the hole in the bottle top and fill it with coloured water.*

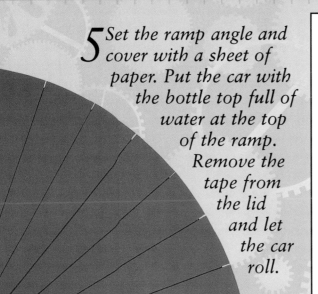

5 Set the ramp angle and cover with a sheet of paper. Put the car with the bottle top full of water at the top of the ramp. Remove the tape from the lid and let the car roll.

LITTLE CAR, BIG CAR

Repeat the project, this time with a heavier car. Does this difference in weight make any difference to the rate of acceleration and the gaps between each of the drops?

WHY IT WORKS

You will see that the spaces between drops become greater as the car moves down the ramp. This is because the car is accelerating, covering a greater distance between the release of each drop. Repeat the project on a steeper slope. The gaps will be even greater, as the car accelerates at an even faster rate.

FINDING OUT MORE

ACCELERATION
This is the rate at which an object moves faster and faster. *Compare different rates of acceleration in the project on pages 28-29.*

AREA This is the amount of space that an object covers. *Turn to pages 10-11 to see how to make your own area grid to find out the area of different shapes.*

CENTRE OF GRAVITY This is an invisible point on an object, through which the weight of the object is said to act. *Find the centre of gravity on a variety of different shapes in the project on pages 20-21.*

DENSITY This is how compact a substance is. Density is measured by the amount, or mass, of the substance which occupies a certain volume.

NERVE SIGNALS

Nerve cells carry signals from your brain to all parts of your body. Signals can travel around the long nerve cells at an astonishing 100m per second.

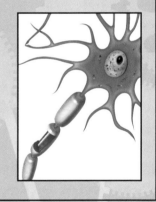

DENSE PLANET

The planet Saturn has such a low density that a piece of it would float in water. A similar chunk of Earth would sink.

Learn how to make your own hydrometer in the project on pages 14-15 and how to compare the densities of different liquids.

TALLEST BUILDINGS

The tallest buildings in the world are the Petronas Towers in Kuala Lumpur in Malaysia. These twin towers measure an amazing 450m high.

DISTANCE This is how far it is between objects. Distance can be measured in centimetres, metres or kilometres. *Make a distance-measuring device on pages 6-7.*

GRADIENT This is a stretch of ground which slopes up or down. *Learn how to make a theodolite on pages 8-9, and use it to measure the angle of slopes.*

PENDULUM This is a weight which swings on the end of a long string or pole. *Find out how a pendulum can be used to measure time on pages 24-25.*

SPEED This is the rate at which an object covers a distance in a particular period of time. *Build a wind-speed reader in the project on pages 26-27 and compare the different speeds of the wind.*

VOLUME This is the amount of space that an object takes up in three directions, called dimensions. *The project on pages 12-13 shows you how to find the volume of different objects.*

BREATHING IN

Your lungs are two sponge-like organs inside your chest, which fill with air every time you take a breath. Everybody needs air to survive. When you take in a very deep breath, your lungs can hold as much as four litres of air.

INDEX

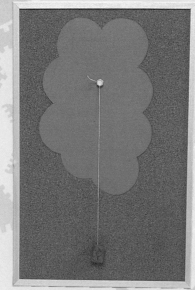